Write it! Publish it! Sell it!

I0415604

Publish it!
How to self-publish your book for free using Kindle Direct Publishing (KDP), CreateSpace and Smashwords

Adam Jackson

Contents

Preface

From the author of *Write it! How to write your book in 30 hours or less* comes this complete guide to self-publishing. By following the steps in this book you can publish a printed or ebook and make it available to readers in as little as 10 minutes.

If you have written or are writing a book and are considering your publishing options then Publish it! is for you. It will show you just how easy it is to self-publish your work, it will provide you with the motivation to get your writing done and it will help you plan your publication strategy.

Publish it! is a complete guide to formatting your book and using online publishing services. It also provides information on other self-publishing options. Publish it! will prove a useful resource each time you self-publish a book or consider self-publishing options for your existing books.

Publish it! follows on from where Write It! leaves off. Publish and start selling your book today.

Introduction

Once upon a time you invested time in writing and perfecting your book, you then sent your manuscript to an agent or publisher and sat back and waited. Eventually you would receive a response – nearly all manuscripts received by agents and publishers were, and still are, rejected. If your book was accepted you then had to wait months for your book to appear on the shelves of bookstores, do much of your own promotion, sign away many of your rights to publish your work elsewhere or in different formats and only receive around 10% royalties for each copy sold.

As we know even after publication very few of these fairy tales have a happily ever after. Many books end up being remaindered and sold off at a considerably reduced price leaving you, as the writer, with very little to show for your hard work.

For years publishers have had the monopoly on who and what gets published, this has also meant they controlled what readers read. Thankfully those days are now long gone and there is a real alternative. The publishing world has radically changed very much in favour of both writers and readers; no longer do publishers decide which genres get published or how many pages a book should have. With the massive growth in ereaders and professional self-publishing services you, as the writer, now have direct access to the reader.

As a bonus you, as the publisher, keep the rights to publish your book elsewhere, decide on the price to ensure you are able to be competitive whilst maximising your earnings, and keep a high percentage (with some options this can be 100%) of royalties or profits from the sales of your books.

For many writers self-publishing is the publishing option of choice rather than a last resort. Much of the industry is now catching up with the fact that self-published books are not second rate, they are high quality, well-written and, more importantly, wanted by readers. Self-published books and writers are now being considered for major book prizes, receive offers for the film rights and are even being offered traditional publishing contracts. It's worth noting that some traditional publishers now offer self-publishing options alongside their traditional contracts.

Self-publishing can be achieved on any budget – you decide the amount you want to spend and the services you wish to purchase – if you choose to do the work yourselves you can even publish on a zero budget.

Sell your work as an ebook on Amazon, Apple iBookstore or Smashwords. Have your own website where you can sell your book as a downloadable *pdf*.

Publish a printed book to sell in your local bookstore, on Amazon, from your website or in your local store.

You have invested a huge amount of your time into writing a book; you want it available to readers and readers want your book. What are you waiting for? Become a published writer today.

1 - Why self-publish?

Self-publishing has become the publication method of choice for many writers; in the past this route, typically known as vanity publishing, was seen as only for those whose work was not good enough to be shared with readers. Well all that has changed; there are self-published books out there that are far superior to books that have been published by mainstream publishers. Readers are now actively seeking out writers that have previously been denied to them.

If you have written a book and want to make it available to readers as soon as possible then self-publishing has significant benefits to both the new and established writer. You can now publish what you write - any genre, any length, short stories, sagas, reports, academic research, comedy or life stories; it's your choice. Let readers decide if there is a viable market for your writing, if you are passionate about your work then you will most likely find others who are too.

You have the option to keep a bigger share of the profits – if you create an ebook and distribute it yourself you keep 100% of all sales, even when using an online retailer to manage the sale and distribution of your book, e.g. Amazon or Smashwords, you keep a substantial percentage of the income from sales.

You have control over the speed of publication – your book can be available to readers in as little as 10 minutes from hitting the *Publish* button. You can quite literally publish and start selling your book today.

You can self-publish for free – publish your book as both a printed and ebook for no upfront costs. This is excellent news for those on a limited budget as you can decide where to allocate your budget or choose to undertake all tasks yourself.

You need no special skills – only basic word-processing and internet skills are needed to format and upload your work; self-publishing services are easy to use.

You keep all of the publishing rights – you decide how to publish your book, where to make it available and when to publish. Keep your book available for as long as you like with no remaindering and no reduced royalties.

You decide the price of your book – ensure your book is both priced competitively and provides you the opportunity to maximise your earnings. Selling at a low price might increase your sales, if there is a limited market for your work then maybe a higher price is better.

You decide to undertake as much or as little of the publishing, promotion and sales tasks as you desire - buy in services you feel are worth paying for either to improve your book or to give yourself more time to devote to your writing.

You have access to a wide range of distribution options – self-publishing services provide distribution channels that include online retailers and high street bookstores. You can also promote your books in retail outlets that might seem less obvious, e.g. your local shop, places of historical interest, at your training and presentation events, and to relevant interest groups. You can also approach your local bookshops as many are only too pleased to stock books by a local writer.

You can make changes to your book during its lifespan – change the price to improve earnings, add pages to promote your new books, add new links to relevant resources or to your website, correct any errors noticed after publication, change the cover, or change the title. At some point you may want to undertake significant changes or updates; all you need to do is publish a new edition.

You design your own promotion strategy – use methods that meet your preferences and those of your readers; blog, tweet, give talks or readings, create a website or use targeted advertising.

If you want to you can even sell your book to a traditional publisher after self-publishing - agents and publishers are now looking to self-published books and offering contracts; sometimes this can be beneficial if you can secure an excellent advance.

In short you have complete control over your book.

If you have written a book that you want to make available to readers then the question is - why would you not self-publish?

2 - Your self-publishing options

You first need to decide which self-publishing options best suit you and your book. Start by asking yourself the following questions and come up with a publishing plan that meets your needs.

Do you want to see your book available as an ebook, printed book or both?
The quickest way to publish your book and start selling is to publish an ebook. Many writers publish an ebook first and then publish a printed version at a later date. Of course if you work as a trainer or public speaker you may well want printed copies of your book to sell at events.

Do you have a budget for publishing or have you decided to undertake all of the tasks yourself?
You may decide to undertake all publishing tasks yourself which will enable you to publish your book and make it available to readers in both printed and ebook formats for no cost. You may decide to buy in services, these can include proofreading and editing, cover design, and storage if you decide to commission a print

run. Make a list of services you would prefer to buy in and then prioritise them.

How much time do you want to allocate to publishing, sales and distribution?
The actual publishing process can be fairly quick, it can take less than an hour, however managing sales and distribution can take up significant time. Decide whether you want more time writing and less time on administration tasks or prefer to undertake much of the work yourself. If you choose to take on sales and distribution you will need to ensure you have storage space for printed books, have time to keep up to date with orders and are able to create a website from which readers can order your books, download your ebooks and make payments.

Where do you want your book to appear for sale? Amazon? Your local book store?
If you want to sell through Amazon, iBookstore, Barnes and Noble and others you will find this easier if you publish using both Amazon and Smashwords.

What quality of printed book do you want?
Some self-publishing services offer limited or no choice in how your printed book will be

produced. CreateSpace, for example, enables you to produce paperback books only, whereas Lulu offers a range of binding options. Decide what you want and then compare your options.

How much do you want to charge for your book?

This might have an impact on your publishing choices – ebooks are straightforward as there are no printing costs to consider – just decide on the price and look at the services and retailers that support your choice. On Amazon there is a minimum selling price of £0.75/$0.99 however you can make your book available from your own website or Smashwords for free. Print on Demand (POD) books will have a higher per copy production cost than printing multiple copies, if you want to keep the price low you may need to consider paying upfront for a print run.

How much time do you want to allocate to promoting your book?

You may enjoy the promotion and marketing side of self-publication or you may prefer to allocate your time to writing. Some self-publishing services provide you with inclusive promotions. Whilst you can choose to publish to all of the available platforms there may be some restrictions, e.g. if you choose to enroll into KDP Select (Kindle) you cannot offer your ebook for sale elsewhere.

Publishing an ebook

In recent years there has been an ebook revolution; readers are consuming ebooks at a phenomenal rate and there is no sign of this trend slowing. Readers can settle down with their ereader, browse books online, make a purchase and start reading within minutes. We live in an instant society; when a buyer makes a purchase they want their item now.

Publishing an ebook is probably the quickest, easiest and cheapest way to get your book in front of your potential readers. There are many other advantages to publishing an ebook; royalties are higher than for printed books (mainly due to cheaper production and delivery costs), readers have instant access to their purchases and publishing is quick and easy.

Ebooks can be read on a computer, laptop, tablet, ereader and mobile phone. Just think of the potential readers you have available to you. With ereaders now available with internet access and a wide range of apps, essentially putting them into the tablet category, they are only going to become more popular.

Ebooks tend to be reasonably priced, even cheap; the result is that readers will give little thought to making that £2.99 purchase perhaps in the same way they give little thought when deciding to buy a cup of coffee. For the writer this means more books sold.

With a number of publishers offering publishing, promotion and distribution services for free, two popular ones are Amazon's KDP and Smashwords, you can literally publish and sell today.

Publishing with Amazon's KDP provides you with up to 70% royalties and some free promotional activity including emails to readers recommending books based on their previous purchases and a "customers also bought" feature.

Publishing with Smashwords provides you with up to 85% royalties and also provides the opportunity to make your book available on Apple iBookstore, Barnes and Noble and other online retailers.

If you wish to sell your book as an ebook through your own distribution channels you can format your book as a *pdf* file (see chapter 4) and sell through your own website or through an online retailer of digital products.

Publishing an ebook has much to offer both the new and experienced writer. Now is the time to benefit from this digital revolution.

Publishing a printed book

For a writer there is nothing quite like holding a physical copy of your book in your hands. Even better is seeing copies of your book on the shelves of bookstores. There are many advantages to publishing a printed book; you can use features that may not display correctly on ereaders, e.g. tables. You control much of the formatting including text type and size. You can sell your book in locations not suited to the sale of ebooks such as your training events or high street stores; and, as with ebooks, you can publish for free.

The cost of producing a printed book is higher than an ebook so you will need to consider your pricing strategy. It is perfectly OK to charge different prices for printed and ebook versions of the same book. In fact there is an advantage to this – readers see the ebook at a significantly lower price and perceive that they are getting excellent value for money.

There are several ways to approach publishing a printed book.

Print on Demand (POD)
This is a quick, easy and often free way to publish a book; as you do not need to invest in a print run you can also test the market. There are many advantages to POD including no storage considerations, no upfront payments for print runs and the ability to change the content of your book without waiting for previous stock to be sold. The main disadvantage is that printing costs can be higher than other methods meaning you may need to charge a higher price for your book or be prepared to take a lower profit margin.

CreateSpace (Amazon) provides writers with a free service which includes promotion and distribution. They will keep an amount of money from the sale of each copy sold; you can set the book price accordingly and so determine your profit.

Lulu is another popular POD service that is easy to use; they will also sell your book from their website. Lulu has the additional advantage of offering you a range of binding and paper options.

Both Amazon and Lulu have additional distribution channels you can buy into.

Print run
Commissioning a long print run (1000+ copies) can significantly reduce the cost of each book. You can either use a self-publishing company or organize the printing yourself through a local or specialist printer.

Which self-publishing service?
Amazon's KDP – a free to use service that enables you to publish your ebook and make it available across all of Amazon's territories; they manage sales and distribution and offer different royalty options based on your pricing. KDP also have a range of promotional tools that support increasing your sales including a "*customers also bought*" section. If you enroll into KDP Select you can promote your book as free for five days in every ninety and you will earn income each time your book is borrowed by Amazon Prime members.

Smashwords – a free to use service offering a range of distribution channels including iBookstore and Barnes and Noble. They will manage sales and distribution and offer royalty options based on distribution channels.

Lulu – a popular free to use POD service that offers you, the writer, a range of binding options. Lulu is a popular POD service that enables you to create a printed book that meets your requirements. Lulu provides a range of options including paper grade, paperback or hardback, colour or black and white. You can choose to pay for the global reach option which will make your book available to bookstores.

Amazon's CreateSpace – another free to use POD service that prints your book as a paperback and makes it available on Amazon. They also offer expanded distribution channels for which there is a cost.

Self-publishing companies - a number of companies offer self-publishing packages. It is important to consider all aspects of printing and selling a printed book in order to decide on the best package for you.

There are some excellent self-publishing companies out there as well as some who charge a lot of money for a poor service (vanity publishers). Good companies will work with you to provide professional advice and services resulting in a package that is tailored to meet your needs.

Typical packages include editing, cover design, ISBN, ebook conversion, promotion to booksellers, managing storage and distribution, and printing an agreed number of your book.

It is worthwhile spending some time getting recommendations, visiting the company premises and inspecting samples of printed books before deciding on which self-publishing company to use. Always check the contract before signing.

Managing the publication process yourself - you can of course manage the whole process yourself and buy in the services you need from separate sources. You might even decide to set up your own publishing company. If you choose this route consider the time you will need to invest managing the publishing process, and sales and distribution. Of course this could be the start of a whole new business, one you enjoy as much as writing.

The choice is yours. Decide on the best approach for you and then start preparing your book for publication.

3 - Preparing your book for publication – completion

You have written your book and want to make it available to readers as quickly as possible. Just before you publish you need to complete a few tasks to ensure it looks great, meets any publishing requirements and is effectively promoted.

You need to edit your book, create a title, create a cover, write a description and blurb, write the front and back matter and then format your work to meet the requirements of your chosen publication method.

If you have followed the steps in *Write it! - how to write your book in 30 hours or less*, you are ready to go to the next chapter and format your book.

Create a title
A great title will grab the attention of readers; this is the first step towards making a purchase.

A carefully crafted title will encourage search engines to propel your book to the first page of search results. Note that the majority of people who search online for products do not look beyond page three; if your book appears after this a reader may never know it exists. If readers don't see it they won't buy it.

Titles are important, many readers will make a purchase based on the title alone, this is particularly true for non-fiction books. If you have written a fiction book you can be creative with your title however ensure you never deceive your reader; remember you want them to buy your future titles. If you have written a non-fiction book your title should reflect the subject matter and support search engines finding your book when someone wants to buy a book on your topic.

One of the best ways to approach creating a title for both fiction and non-fiction books is to create a short title, which might be creative, followed by a sub-title, which should be descriptive. Think about the words and phrases that potential readers might type into a search engine to find the type of book you have written – try and incorporate these words and phrases into your sub-title. You can decide whether or not to include the sub-title on the cover of your book, however ensure you include it everywhere else to maximise impact.

Consider these examples of titles with sub-titles. Both are fairly short though you can see how the sub-title might improve search engine optimisation.

Steam – a history of steam engines in trains and machinery during the 19th century.

Life (Thriller set on Death Row).

If you are publishing your book as an ebook or using POD it is easy to change the title if you find the book is not making the desired sales.

Create a cover

Never judge a book by its cover! Of course that is exactly what everyone does. Your cover needs to be eye-catching and look professional. Your cover should attract the reader and encourage them to read your description or blurb.

Many writers choose to outsource their cover design; you can use online services, a local designer, or try your local college and see if any students would like a live project. Always supply a detailed brief to ensure the cover reflects the theme and content of your book because your cover is a key selling tool.

A free alternative is to use online cover creators which are available with some online publishing services, e.g. CreateSpace, these include easy to use templates and access to high quality images. If you are using a self-publishing company they may offer cover design as part of the package.

If you have the design skills or a limited budget then create the cover yourself using photo-editing software; there is excellent software available for free. You can take your own photos to use with your design or purchase images online for a reasonable price; ensure any purchased images are royalty free.

If you are taking the DIY approach the key to creating an attractive cover is to keep it simple:
 - Use no more than three different font types.
 - Use images that represent the general topic, theme, setting or characters of your book.
 - Ensure that any text can be read over the chosen image. Of course you may decide not to use images at all.
 - Ensure the edge of your book is dark, add a thin, dark border if necessary. This will ensure your book stands out when displayed online as it is likely to be displayed against a white background.

- Image size is important for both epublishing and printing. It is important to check the requirements of each publisher. For epublishing a picture width of a minimum 1400 pixels with a ratio of 1:1.6 works well. For printed books your image size will be based on your book size so select your book size first and set your image size accordingly. For printed books your cover will include the back and spine.

- As a final check ensure your cover looks attractive in greyscale.

Keep notes about your cover design as you may need to recreate it; it is often easier to recreate your cover than to make changes to an existing image.

Note: if you intend to use an online cover creator it is useful to prepare your images and produce a mock-up of your cover before you publish.

Write a blurb and description
The purpose of both the blurb and description is to ensure readers make a purchase; after reading these they will either decide not to buy or add the book to their basket. These are your prime marketing tools – use them well.

Generally the blurb goes on the back of your printed book and the description will be displayed on your book's online sales pages. Whilst the same text can be used for both you could be missing a huge promotion opportunity if you do not make best use of a description. Both can be used on other promotional material - press release, blog, website, advert or leaflet.

The blurb is usually a paragraph or two in length and is used to entice the reader to read more e.g. *"Following the death of her father Mary returns to her family home to sell the house and tie up loose ends. Little did she realise the long held secrets she would discover that would rock her understanding of who she was and put her life in danger."*

The description is often longer and provides more information about your book; it can include the blurb. As the description is used online - retailers, your website and review sites - it is important to use as many keywords and phrases that might be used by those searching for a book like yours. *"Are you looking to start a home-based business," "collecting teddy bears."* Using relevant search engine friendly phrases in your description will get your book displayed when readers are looking for your type of book.

If your potential readers never see your book they will never buy it; the description is one of your most powerful promotional tools. Spend some time thinking about what a reader might enter when looking for a book like yours; obviously do not deceive your readers but collecting teddy bears might include a reference to antiques, toys, dolls houses, gifts, car boot sales, eBay, days out, visiting historic houses and more.

Your writing should stand out – the blurb will entice the reader to read more, the description is a sales page to make them hit the *"Buy Now"* button.

Write your front matter
Front matter is the additional information that goes at the beginning of your book. If you are publishing both an ebook and a printed book, or a using a number of different publishing services, you may need slightly different versions to meet minimum requirements. Front matter should include:
Title – both the main title and sub-title
Author – your name or pen name

Publisher – either your name, your pen name or a publisher name if you set up a publishing company

Copyright - use the symbol or the word copyright followed by owner of the copyright (author name/pen name) and year of first publication

ISBN – required for printed books, whilst this is not essential for ebooks you may need one to sell through some online retailers

Kindle or Smashwords Edition - for ebooks you may require these words depending on the publishing service chosen.

Take a look at the beginning of this book to see how little is actually required.

You may decide to include additional front matter such as a legal statement, acknowledgements, dedications, credits, foreword or edition number.

Note: If you publish to Amazon's Kindle or Smashwords then your book will have an additional promotional tool – *"See inside"* or *"Sample"* – a number of pages will be made available for readers to preview and download. Try not to clutter up the available sample pages with front matter; you should use this promotional tool to its best advantage and ensure that what readers see encourages them to buy. Once you have met the minimum requirements for front matter then you could choose to place everything else at the back of your book.

Add back matter

You may wish to add additional material at the end of your book; this could include material that supports your book such as a glossary. It is most useful for promoting other books you have written, your website, blog, social media information and other services you offer.

Create promotional pages for each of your books, you can use the description and reviews for this, include how to buy information, this should include a clickable link in an ebook or the full website address in printed books, never use clickable affiliate links as some retailers do not allow these. Remove any price details as you may change these over time.

Promote your next book, even if you have not yet written it. It is a good idea to give a publication date as this gives readers something to look forward to, creates anticipation, and also gives you a deadline. Once you have published your next book remember to update this promotional page to include the new details.

Promote books by other writers; this could be a reciprocal arrangement whereby they also promote your work. In most cases you are not in competition with other writers, people buy more of what they like rather than selecting just one book from a category. Promoting in this way can align you with other successful writers.

Create a page to promote your other activities including your website, blog and your business, for instance you may be a consultant, guest speaker or trainer. Give people a reason to read your blog, tell them the benefits, e.g. "*I will post details of book promotions here*" or "*hints and tips on ways to make extra money*". As before add a link or provide website information.

These pages are an excellent opportunity for you to promote yourself – make use of them.

Set the price

Price matters. Price can have a huge impact on both sales and income earned from both this book and other books you write; it can be beneficial to have a pricing strategy that might include price changes during the lifespan of your book.

Price too low and readers may perceive your book as having little value. Price too high and you may limit your market.

Consider your goals. Do you want to sell high volumes of books in order to get your name known and therefore create a loyal following that will be prepared to pay higher prices for your future books, or do you want to maximise your income from this one book?

Your goals may change throughout the lifespan of your book. Often writers reduce the price of a book when they publish a new book, perhaps the next in a series; readers buy the first at a reduced price and then go on to buy the next book at a higher price. This is a strategy that can be successful and increase your total book sales and income.

There will be a minimum price you need to charge, though you may be prepared to make short term losses in order to promote this or other books. If you are publishing a printed book you will price based on your production costs (including service provider costs), and then add an amount which becomes your profit.

If you have invested in a print run you may also want to consider how many books you are likely to sell initially, use this as the basis for covering your production costs. If you think you will easily sell 150 books then price to cover all of your costs with the sale of 150 books, you start making a profit from the sale of book number 151.

If you are publishing an ebook you will need to check the publishing service/retailer guidelines. If you publish to Amazon's Kindle using KDP you should have a minimum price of £0.75/$0.99 however, to achieve 70% royalties, you will need to price at between £1.49/$2.99 - £6.99/$9.99. When selling on Amazon you cannot offer your ebook at a cheaper price elsewhere. Amazon do not allow you to publish with a zero price however you can use their promotion scheme to offer your book for free for five days in ninety. Some writers make use of Amazon's price match; they offer their book for free elsewhere and then wait until Amazon also sets the price to zero. Think carefully before taking this approach as you may be in breach of Amazon's terms and conditions.

The production costs for printed books will be higher than for ebooks, because of this you may decide to charge different prices for the different formats. There can be an advantage to doing this as the reader will perceive the ebook as being excellent value if considerably cheaper than the printed version.

Over time you may choose to experiment with the price to maximize earnings. For example if you sell 1000 copies of your book for £0.99 at 35% royalties you earn a little under £350. If you sell 100 copies at £6.99 at 70% royalties then your income will be just under £500. Get this right and you can maximize your profits.

Edit
Your text should be as close to error free as possible when you publish, however if you are publishing an ebook or using POD and you, or your proofreader, miss anything you can

always make changes and republish at a later date.

It is useful to make several passes of your book, each with a different purpose; this enables you to focus on the task rather than skimming through the text as if you are a reader.

Read your work aloud, this will help your notice where the words don't flow.

Check for unnecessary adverbs and adjectives, remove them, and if necessary look for a stronger verb or noun e.g. instead of "*he ran very fast*" try "*he sprinted*". You can use a thesaurus for this.

Check spelling – if you are uncertain use a dictionary, or change the word. Ensure you check for common misspellings – there, their, they're. Spell-check may not pick these up.

Check punctuation – misplaced apostrophes are the bane of readers' lives. If unsure rewrite the sentence.

Check all links in ebooks – make sure they work. It is useful to include the web address in full as well as a "*click here*" link. This will help readers locate the webpage or site.

Check facts – if you are using factual information then check it with at least three sources.

Save a master copy
Save a copy of your book and name it *xxxfinaledited.doc.*

When your book is completed save a Master copy as a read only file to ensure you do not accidently overwrite during the formatting for publication process.

If, at a later stage, you need to make some changes, e.g. you find a spelling error, make the changes on this Master and then start the process of formatting for publication again to ensure all copies are the same.

You are now ready to format and publish your book.

4 - Preparing your book for publication - formatting

To ensure your book looks great on all ereaders and in print you need to format it to meet the requirements of your chosen publishing method and to ensure the contents of your book are correctly displayed or printed.

To format your book you can use any word-processor that enables you to save as *doc*, *pdf* and *html*. This need not involve expensive software purchases; both LibreOffice and OpenOffice are free to download and do the job nicely. If you need to convert your book into other formats, for example *ePub*, you will find online conversion tools, often these are provided by the self-publishing service.

Note: if you intend to sell your ebook from your website or through a digital products retailer you will probably want to format your book as a *pdf*. If this is the case follow the instructions for formatting a printed book, the *pdf* is designed to be read online as well as printed. Set your page size to A4 or to a standard print paper size.

Formatting your ebook

One of the benefits of ereaders is that users have considerable control over the way text is displayed; this includes font size, type and colour. This means you should create a document that contains minimal formatting to ensure your book looks great when read.

The conversion process from word-processed document to ereader format may ignore some of your applied formatting; in fact different ereader formats may behave in different ways. Your book needs to look great even if all of the formatting is removed. To ensure your book looks great you need to follow one rule – Keep it Simple.

Styles – many ereaders support styles, in fact some conversions make use of them however, you need to keep these simple. Use Normal, Heading 1 and Heading 2; you can use Heading 3 if needed but any more than this may have a negative impact on the conversion. Modify the styles if necessary to suit your needs. Set Normal to Arial font size 12, Heading 1 (for chapter headings) to Arial font size 14, bold and centred, Heading 2 (for subheadings) to font size 12 and bold. Bold and align centre usually display as formatted.

Do not apply colour as this will not display on black and white ereaders.

Font type, size and colour – you can apply formatting directly to the text, always use a standard font type such as Arial, Times New Roman or Garamond, and remember the user can change this to suit their preferences. Keep the same font type throughout your book and only change the size for chapter headings and sub-headings. Colour should be set to black or automatic.

Emphasis – italics, bold and underline are usually preserved. Leave these in your text however ensure the text is easy to follow if these are removed or changed.

Spacing between words – use one space only between each word, this includes spacing after a full stop. Additional spaces may be removed in the conversion process. A quick way to replace two spaces with one space is to use your word-processor's find and replace feature; in the find box press the space bar twice, in the replace box press the spacebar once. Select replace all and the job is done.

Paragraphs – decide to either use an indent at the start of each new paragraph OR a line space between paragraphs; do not use both for the same paragraph. Typically an indent is used for fiction and a line space is used for non-fiction however the choice is yours. If you decide to use an indent you should use the first line indent formatting feature, do not use the space bar or tabs. Select all of your text, select format paragraph and set first line indent to 0.5cm.

Note: if you have a line space after a chapter heading you should remove the indent from that first paragraph.

Bullets and automatic numbering – these may not be supported on the ereader so remove automatic bullets and numbering and replace these with manually entered numbers.

Return/Enter key – when you press the return key you start a new paragraph and paragraph formatting e.g. first line indent, is applied. However some ebook conversions will ignore all but the first hard return and remove any line spacing you have created. If you want to put additional line spaces between text use *Shift+Return* to create a forced line break. If you need to preserve any paragraph formatting, e.g. first line indent, then use the *Return* key on its own for the final line space.

Alignment – with the exception of text formatted as centred, e.g. chapter headings, all text should be left aligned or justified. The ereader will have a default display setting which, in some cases, can be controlled by the user. It is likely that the ereader will display the text as justified.

Tabs – many ereaders do not support them; use the first line indent feature to indent if required.

Tables – these are not currently supported by many ereaders. If you have created a table that is vital to your book, reproduce and insert it as an image.

Columns – these may not display correctly on most ereaders. It is better to remove the columns however if you believe that retaining the columns is essential then reproduce and insert as an image. Aim to keep the text content in images at a minimum as you may lose some of the clarity.

Page breaks – these work on some ereaders and are ignored by others. If you are publishing to multiple ereaders and do not want to create separate files for each one you can overcome this by inserting a page break immediately after the last sentence of a chapter and then inserting a maximum of four forced line breaks before starting the next chapter. If the page breaks is recognised then the next chapter will start partway down the next page, this is perfectly acceptable and sometimes preferred. If the page break is ignored there will be a reasonable space between the two chapters.

Headers and footers – remove these along with any page numbering.

Line spacing - set line spacing between 1 and 1.5, as with other formatting this may be managed by the ereader. Set the before and after paragraph spacing to 0.

Emphasis – use bold, italics and/or underline with consistency.

Colour – some ereaders are black and white only, others give the user control over text colour. Use black only for text and ensure images are clear when displayed in greyscale.

Images - ensure images look good when displayed in greyscale. You may need to consider file size of the images, e.g. when publishing to Kindle the maximum image size is 127KB.

Note: during the conversion process your images may be saved as separate files, you just need to remember this if you are saving or moving files into new locations on your computer – remember to move the image files and maintain any folder structure.

Links – these are supported as long as the ereader supports web browsing and is connected to the internet. It can be helpful to provide the web address as well as a *click here* option. Test all links to ensure they work correctly.

Step by step - formatting your ebook

1) Open your edited document. Save the document as *xxxfinalebookformatted.doc*. Do not overwrite your edited master as you may need it later. Save your work regularly.

2) Add your ebook front matter to the beginning of your book.

3) Change text to a standard font type and size, e.g. Arial, size 12, either directly or by using styles.

4) Apply font size and emphasis formatting as required, e.g. chapter headings, either directly or using styles.

5) Set line spacing to between 1 and 1.5, if required set first line indent to 0.5cm, set spacing before and after paragraph to 0 and alignment to left aligned or justified (paragraph formatting).

6) Remove headers, footers and page numbering.

7) Turn on show/hide (Pilcrow) button to show all non-printing characters.

8) Remove all tabs, replace with first line indent if required.

9) Remove additional spaces between words.

10) Remove automatic bullets and numbering; replace manually as required.

11) Remove additional hard returns and replace with soft/forced returns where more than one line space is required.

12) Remove first line indent from first paragraph of each chapter if you have entered a line space between chapter heading and the first paragraph.

13) Check page breaks are placed immediately after the last word or punctuation mark of each chapter. If required add extra line spaces using a soft/forced return at the end of each chapter.

14) Centre chapter headings if required.

15) Add and test internal and external links.

16) Save.

This file will now be used to publish your book. As different services require different file formats at this stage save as a *doc* file, you will convert at the publishing stage.

You are now ready to publish your ebook.

Formatting your printed book

Publishing a printed book opens up extensive markets to writers; bookshops can stock and sell your book and you can sell copies at your talks or teaching sessions.

If you are going to sell through online retailers such as Amazon then the quickest and cheapest (no upfront costs) way to get started is to use a Print on Demand (POD) service that prints and binds each copy as it is ordered. The production cost per book is higher than commissioning a print run however you do not need to invest in printing and storing multiple copies.

Most POD services prefer or require the book to be formatted as a *pdf* file. This gives you considerable control over the way the book looks as you can make use of more formatting features. It is however important to comply with submission requirements, which mainly relate to trim size and margins, else your book may be rejected or may not print correctly.

Before you start you need to decide on the size of your book; you can then set up the correct page/trim size. It is better to use a standard size, there are several, as some stores may not stock books of a non-standard size. Also check any sizing constraints relating to other options including paper colour and binding.

I would recommend downloading and using templates available from POD services such as

Amazon's CreateSpace or Lulu. These templates will enable you to import your text (copy and paste) to a template that is set up with the correct page size and margins; some templates include guidance on content and formatting, e.g. front matter and font types. Take a look at those available at https://www.createspace.com/en/community/docs/DOC-1323

Font type – because this is a printed book you can select the font type, however you still need to keep this simple. You also need to check that the font will embed correctly, the font is freely available for you to use and that it will look good when printed; some fonts look fine on screen but poor when printed; stick to the tried and tested such as Times New Roman, Arial or Garamond. Generally speaking a serif font type is better for printed books however sans serif can work well for young children.

Font size – set to 11 or 12, do a sample print to see how this looks. You can set chapter headings to a larger font size, 14 works well however you may want to experiment with up to size 16.

Note: when you set up your document using a POD service you may find that there is a slight variation on the printed font size as the pages may be "*fit to page*" if there is not an exact page size match.

Styles – the settings are preserved when converting to *pdf*. Keep styles simple and use only standard font types. Set up styles for your body text, chapter headings, sub-headings and any other blocks of text that require a specific look.

Alignment – Most printed books are fully justified. If you prefer you can left align, this can improve readability in books designed for young children.

Drop capitals – decide if you would like to use drop capitals at the start of each chapter, these will be preserved when converting to *pdf.*

Line spacing – set this between 1 and 1.2. This looks professional and helps keep cost down as an increase in line spacing equals more pages. Set spacing before and after paragraphs to 0.

Page breaks – insert page breaks at the end of each chapter and anywhere else you think a page break will improve layout.

Paragraphs – decide to either use an indent at the start of each new paragraph OR a line space between paragraphs; do not use both for the same paragraph. Typically an indent is used for fiction and a line space is used for non-fiction however the choice is yours. If you decide to use an indent you should use the first line indent formatting feature, do not use the space bar or tabs. Select all of your text, select format paragraph and set first line indent to 0.5cm.

Note: if you have a line space after a chapter heading you should remove the indent from that first paragraph.

Margins – set as required, this will most likely be determined by your publishing service; check their guidelines or use their template. Remember the inner margin will need to be slightly wider than the outer margin to allow for binding, this is known as the gutter. You will need to mirror margins as you are printing on both sides of the paper. As a guideline set the outer, top and bottom margin to 0.5in and the inner margin to 0.75in, this includes an amount for the gutter.

Note: measurements are given in inches as this tends to be used by the industry.

Headers, footers and page numbers – you are able to use headers, footers and page numbering in printed books, in fact you should always include page numbers. You may want to include the chapter name in the header, perhaps the author name in the footer, and you could use solid lines to separate the header from the body of the text. Have a look at some examples of books that make good use of headers and footers and then decide how you want yours to look.

Tables – *pdf* files support tables, ensure they fit on the page when you have reduced the page size down to your required book size.

Tabs – these are supported when converting to *pdf,* as with tables ensure these still look good when the page size is reduced.

Columns – you are able to use columns with a printed book; aim for each column to be at least five words wide, unless a list, as this improves readability.

Bullets and numbering – you can use automatic numbering and add bullet points to your book.

Images – ensure your image will print clearly when resized to fit your page or the space allocated to it. If you are not printing in colour then convert your image to greyscale before you insert it into your book.

Colour – books can be printed in colour however this will add to the cost. If you decide to print in black and white or greyscale then change font colour to black or grey and convert images to greyscale.

Links – as this is a printed book links will need to be removed, you should replace any *click here* links with the full web address, e.g.

https://www.google.co.uk, you may also need to reword the text explaining the link.

Step by step - formatting your printed book

1) Open your master document and save as *xxxformatforprint.doc* (you will convert to a *pdf* at the end).

2) Set the page size as required and set your margins to 0.5in for top, bottom and outside edge and 0.75in for the inside edge (to be bound). You should then mirror margins as you will be printing on both sides of the paper.

OR

1) Open a book size template and save as *xxxformatforprint.doc*.

2) Import/copy and paste the text from your master document into the template.

AND

3) Add your front and back matter.

Note: you will require an ISBN for printed books.

4) Add page breaks where needed.

5) Use styles or directly apply formatting to your text, e.g. font size, type and emphasis, ensure consistency of formatting for body text, headings, quotes and thoughts.

6) Add headers, footers and page numbers.

7) Set line spacing between 1 and 1.2.

8) Set alignment to left align or fully justified.

9) Centre text as required, e.g. chapter headings.

10) Add additional emphasis (italics, bold, underline) as required.

11) Add bullet points and numbering, format these as required.

12) Check images are correctly placed.

13) Remove any links and ensure web addresses are written in full.

14) Save your changes.

15) Save as a *pdf* file ensuring that you embed images and fonts.

16) Open your new document in a *pdf* reader to ensure all text and formatting is displayed as intended. Make changes if required.

Your book is now ready to publish.

5 - Publishing

You now have a formatted manuscript ready to publish. Unless you have a particular reason to produce a printed book first I would recommend publishing an ebook. This gives you the opportunity to see your book available to buy in a just a few hours or even in just a few minutes.

Publishing to Amazon's Kindle using KDP

Amazon's Kindle is the market leader in e-readers, books can be read on a Kindle and Kindle apps enabling readers to purchase and read books on their ereader, mobile phone, tablet, or computer. Once you have gone through the publication process your book will usually be available on the Amazon website within 12 hours.

KDP allows you to upload and publish from a variety of formats including *doc, html, pdf, txt,* and other formats. It can be useful to convert your document to the *prc* format prior to publishing as, at the time of writing, this enables you to thoroughly check your book on a Kindle or Kindle app prior to publication; this makes it easier to see any formatting errors.

Mobipocket Creator can be used to convert your book into the *prc* format.

If you prefer you can skip this next stage and go straight to the next section - Publishing with KDP.

Step by step – creating a *prc* file using Mobipocket Creator

1) Download and install a copy of Mobipocket Creator from www.mobipocket.com

Note: this is currently only available for PCs

2) Open your formatted for ebook file - *xxxfinalebookformatted.doc* - and save as a *Web Page Filtered* or *html* file. You will need it in this format whether you use Mobipocket Creator first or go straight to KDP.

3) Open Mobipocket Creator.

4) From the list under *Import From Existing File* select *HTML Document*.

5) Browse for your saved *html* document, select and click *Import.*

6) Click on *Cover Image*, located in the list on the left. Click *Add cover image*.

7) Browse for and select the image.

8) ***Important*** - scroll to the bottom on the page and click *Update*.

9) Using the options on the left side of the screen you can add a table of contents and

metadata however these are not essential. If you choose to add metadata check each box is filled in correctly as some information has to be entered in a specific way, e.g. the author name is entered as surname, first name.

10) Scroll to the bottom of the screen and click *Update*.

11) From the icons along the top of the screen click *Build* and then *Build*.

12) If you get any error messages read these and correct. The most common one occurs because you have not clicked on *Update* after selecting a cover image or adding metadata.

13) When Build has finished click on *Open Folder* and then *OK*.

14) You now have a *prc* file ready to copy to your Kindle content folder.

15) If you are using your computer and have downloaded Kindle for PC you will have a folder called *My Kindle Content*; copy the *prc* file into this folder.

OR

15) If you want to copy the file onto a Kindle, connect it to your computer via a USB port and copy the *prc* file into the Kindle's document folder.

AND

16) Turn on your Kindle or open Kindle for PC and your book will be available to read, do not

worry if the cover is not displayed, this will be fine when published through KDP.

17) Thoroughly check through your book and look for formatting errors.

18) Correct formatting errors in your formatted for ebook Word file; any spelling errors should be corrected in the Master as well as the formatted version. Save as *Web Page Filtered* or *html* and convert to *prc* using Mobipocket Creator.

19) Repeat until you are happy with the way your book is displayed.

You are now ready to publish to Amazon Kindle store using KDP.

Step by step – publish using KDP

1) If you have not already done so open your formatted for ebook file - *xxxfinalebookformatted.doc* - and save as a *Web Page Filtered* or *html* file.

2) Go to http://kdp.amazon.com/, this will take you to the sign in page.

3) Sign in or create an account.

4) Once you have signed into KDP click on the bookshelf tab.

5) Select *Add new title*.

Note: you are now presented with a screen where you enter information relating to your book, some is mandatory, some optional. Remember that everything you enter will appear on your Amazon sales page so check spellings and ensure the information you enter is what you want to be displayed. At any time you can scroll to the bottom of the first screen and *Save as draft*. You can then return and complete the information later. If you have followed the steps to prepare for publication you will have everything you need.

6) Enter the title – what you write here will appear on Amazon. You can add additional text that does not appear on the cover; this may be useful to the reader or support them finding your book, e.g. you might enter (Thriller) in brackets after your title.

7) If this book is part of a series you can enter this information, you can also enter an edition number.

8) Enter or copy and paste your book description. If you copy and paste check this is formatted as required as you may find some formatting has been removed.

9) Add the contributors, you need to add at least one contributor – author name – however you may add others, e.g. illustrators. Enter the author name as on your book; if using a pen name then enter this.

10) Select the language.

11) Enter the publication date.

12) Enter the publisher name, if you do not have a publishing company set up you can either use your own name, author name or leave this blank.

13) Enter the ISBN, if you do not have one then leave blank. Currently an ISBN is not required for ebooks; Amazon will assign an ASIN to your book.

14) Verify your publishing rights.

15) Categorise your book. This is important as buyers are able to search for "*other books in this category.*" You need to select the most appropriate for your book however have a look at which categories books similar to yours are published in; these are indicated on Amazon near the bottom of a book's sales page.

16) Add keywords and phrases; you can enter up to seven words or strings of words. Think about what buyers might enter when looking for a book like yours.

17) Browse for and upload your book cover.

18) Select your DRM option; this is one option that cannot be changed later.

19) Browse for your book file - *xxxfinalebookformatted.html*.

20) Upload your book.

21) You now have the option to preview your book. This is recommended.

22) Select *Save and Continue;* note that you can *Save as draft* if you want to complete the publishing process at a later date.

23) Verify your publishing territories; if this is your own work then you can select all.

24) Select your royalty rate based on your price.

25) Enter your price – you do need to price in dollars however for other territories/countries you can either input a price or base on the US price. VAT is added to this price in some countries.

26) Opt in or out of lending.

27) Accept terms and conditions.

28) *Save and publish.*

Congratulations, you have completed the publication process and your book is now in review. If your book is written in English it takes up to 12 hours for your book to be available on Amazon, other languages take a little longer. You will receive an email notifying you that your book has been successfully published.

Once you have received your email go to Amazon and Kindle store, search for your book and check through all the details on the sales page. If you see any errors note these and make changes through KDP.

If you need to make changes you can log into KDP, go to bookshelf, click the check box beside your book title, click on the actions drop down list and select the appropriate action.

You can change anything except DRM. Each time you *Save and publish* your book will go back into review; it will remain for sale on Amazon during this time. If you make significant changes to your book content you can ask Amazon to contact previous buyers and offer them an updated version.

The KDP dashboard
When you sign into KDP you can use the dashboard to add new titles and make changes to your existing books. You can also access reports on book sales and royalties. It may be worthwhile saving the monthly sales reports to your computer so that you can use them to analyse trends or impact of promotions.

Once you have signed in to KDP you can access your account details; you will need to complete the section on how you wish to receive your royalties – cheque or electronic transfer (EFT). You will find the information you need for EFT on your bank statement.

KDP Select

KDP Select provides you with the opportunity to offer potential readers promotional offers – currently you can offer your book as free for up to five in every ninety days, you also earn money when your book is borrowed by Amazon Prime customers. If you decide to enroll onto KDP Select you can't offer a digital copy of your book for sale elsewhere.

Additional Resources

There is an excellent free guide available from the Kindle store and on the KDP website; this contains links to up-to-date pricing information, and terms and conditions.

Publish using Smashwords

If you want to make your ebook available through a number of different online retailers then publishing with Smashwords enables you to sell your book in the Smashwords store, Apple iBookstore, Kobo, Barnes and Noble and others.

When publishing to Smashwords you need to provide your document as a Word document; use your *xxxfinalebookformatted.doc* file. Don't worry if you don't use Word as many word-processors can save as *doc*, use the *Save As* feature.

Smashwords puts your document through the Meatgrinder and then churns out your work in the various formats required by the different devices, apps and retailers. As long as you have formatted your book according to the guidelines in chapter 4 then the conversion process should work well however you do need to check each version in case you have left in formatting that causes your book to display incorrectly.

Note: you cannot publish public domain work through Smashwords, only work you have created yourself.

Step by step – publish using Smashwords
1) Go to http://www.smashwords.com/ and then click on *How to Publish on Smashwords.*
2) Create a free account by entering the details required – email address, screen name and password.
3) You will receive an email – click on the link within this email.
4) This verifies your account and redirects you to the Smashwords website. In future you can login directly from the Smashwords homepage.

5) Click *Publish.*

6) Enter the book title, short description and long description. You can copy and paste these if you have prepared them.

7) Select the language and indicate whether or not your book contains adult material.

8) Set the price of your book, allow readers to set price or set your book as free.

Note: when pricing your book take into account any pricing policy for the different retailers, e.g. iBookstore has a pricing policy that requires ebooks to be priced at $x.99 – your book price will be rounded up if necessary.

9) Enable sampling and set the percentage you would like to be made available to readers.

10) Select the primary and secondary categories.

11) Enter the keywords for your book; remember these will support your book being found when readers search online.

12) Select the formats you would like your book converted into, at a minimum select *ePub*, *Kindle* and *pdf*, however you can select them all.13) Browse for and upload your cover image.

14) Browse for and upload your book file (*doc*).

15) Click *Publish.*

16) As soon as conversion is complete your book is available on Smashwords; this can take 2 – 10 minutes.

17) You will receive an email stating your book has been converted; this email will also contain details of any errors you need to correct before your book can be accepted into the Premium Catalog.

18) Once conversion is complete you can access the dashboard to update your book, manage pricing and manage ISBNs (these are available free from Smashwords). If you want your book accepted into the Premium Catalog look at *Premium Status* to check any actions required.

Note: it is advantageous to meet the requirements of the Premium Catalog as once accepted your book will automatically be distributed to online retailers such as Kobo, iBookstore, WHSmith, and Barnes and Noble. You will need to ensure correct formatting, have a professional looking cover, create an appropriate title, use upper and lowercase letters correctly and have a copyright page that identifies the author as the copyright holder. If you follow the preparation requirements in chapters 3 and 4 you should meet these requirements. If there are any errors you can resubmit your book with amendments.

Smashwords dashboard

You can go to your dashboard on Smashwords and upload a new version of your book, change pricing, manage ISBNs, manage distribution channels, check sales and publish new titles.

Additional resources

As with many of the ebook publishers Smashwords has produced excellent guidelines on how to prepare your book for publication.

Publishing using Amazon's CreateSpace

CreateSpace is an Amazon company that enables you to publish printed copies of your book using their online service. You can publish for free; they also offer a range of paid for services. The process is quick and easy with a step by step approach. After you have published you can sell your books through your own author platform, on Amazon, through other retailers and at your own events. Using CreateSpace you can sign up for wider distribution of your book including making your book available through bookstores and online retailers.

Print on demand (POD) means that your book is always in stock – readers don't have to wait until you print another batch. Whilst the per book cost will be more expensive than a large print run you do not need to invest in stock, pay for storage or risk poor sales of your book. It also means if you later come across an error (not an excuse for poor editing as you may get poor reviews) or want to make changes and add updates to produce a 2nd edition you do not have to worry about disposing of unsold stock.

CreateSpace provides a cover creator that enables you to create a professional looking cover using either your own images or those selected from the Image Gallery.

You select the price based on a minimum price calculated from production costs and Amazon's per book fees; this effectively means you are choosing how much you earn in royalties.

CreateSpace prefers your book to be formatted as a *pdf.* There is a tool within CreateSpace to convert *doc* or *rtf* to *pdf* however I would recommend you follow the instructions in chapter 4 to format and convert your book to *pdf* prior to publication.

Step by step - publish using CreateSpace

1) Go to https://www.createspace.com/

2) Login or create an account.

3) Select *Add New Title*.

4) Enter your project title, select *Paperback* and then select *Guided*; use *Expert* when you feel confident publishing with CreateSpace.

5) Enter the book title, subtitle, author details, and contributors. Make use of the *"What's this?"* feature if you require additional advice and guidance on how to enter details correctly.

6) If your book is part of a series then check the series box and enter the series title and volume number.

7) Enter the edition number, 1 if this is the first time you have published this book.

8) Select the language and enter the publication date.

9) Click *Save & Continue.*

10) Choose an ISBN option; CreateSpace will assign one free of charge or you can provide your own. When you have made your choice you will be asked to either enter your ISBN details or click *Assign Free ISBN*.

11) Click *Continue.*

12) Select your interior type, black and white or full colour, your paper colour and your trim size.

Note: colour will add to production costs; cream paper is only available with selected trim sizes. If your *pdf* is not an exact match for your selected trim size you will have a choice of *shrink to fit* or *flowing* the text. If you have set your page size the same as the trim size then select *shrink to fit* when asked as there should be little variation between the two sizes.

13) Select *Upload your Book File.*

14) Click *Browse,* locate and upload *xxxformatforprint.pdf.*

15) Select your preferred bleed option; this determines whether or not images are printed to the edge of the page.

16) Ensure the *Run automated print checks* box is checked.

17) Click *Save.*

18) Click *Launch Interior Reviewer.*

19) Go through each of your pages and note any identified issues; these are identified by a red balloon with a white cross, click on the cross for information on the issue. You can either ignore issues or go back and make changes.

20) When you are satisfied with your book click *Save/Ignore Issues and Save.*

21) Click *Continue/Ignore Issues and Continue.*

22) Select your cover option; you will be asked to either browse for and upload your own cover or click *Launch Cover Creator.* If this is your first use then using the Cover Creator will simplify the task.

Note: If you use the Cover Creator you will first select a design and add elements as required. It is a step by step process. If you do not require some of the elements you can uncheck the *visible* box. You have the option to upload your own images or use those available. The barcode will be added for you. When done click *Submit Cover.*

23) Click *Complete Cover.*

24) Click *Continue.*

25) Click *Submit Files for Review.*

26) You will receive an email within 24 hours with information on the next steps. Whilst you are waiting you need to set up your distribution channels, pricing and book description (including keywords). To do this go back to the *Member Dashboard* and click on the title of your book. You will see actions available to you for this book; they include *Setup, Review* and *Distribute*. In the *Distribute* box you will find the options you still need to complete. Click on the required option and complete details as required. Ensure you have completed your

account details else you will not be able to access pricing and distribution options.

27) Once you have received an email you can either order a proof copy of your book or check the online proof copy. Undertake a thorough check and, if necessary, make changes and upload the amended copy. When you are happy with your book you then approve your proof and your book will be available to purchase.

Congratulations, you now have a printed book available to readers.

Don't forget you can order books yourself to sell at your own events or use for promotional purposes.

CreateSpace dashboard

The Member Dashboard provides access to publishing tools and reports on sales and royalties. You will need to complete your account details before your book can go live.

Additional resources

CreateSpace has a section containing free resources; here you will find a wide range of articles and reports on marketing, formatting, creating content and a useful blog.

Having followed the instructions in this chapter you will have published a printed book, an ebook or both; your book will now be available for sale through online retailers. You are now ready to start actively promoting your book to maximize your book sales and income from royalties.

6 - Promoting your book

You've written it, you've published it, you now need to sell it! Any published writer will tell you that making your book available to the public does not equal sales. You need to actively promote your book on an ongoing basis to maximise sales and income. At this stage readers do not know who you are or even that your book exists; you must tell them.

If you are publishing your ebook exclusively on Amazon Kindle then enroll onto KDP Select and make use of the five promotion days. During this period your book will be made available as free to download. Now you might think that giving your book away is not a good idea, how are you ever going to make money if you charge nothing?

Give it away and you will get significant downloads across all Amazon sites, this increases the chances of getting reviews, your ranking will go up, when a reader looks at a similar book they will see your book in the "*customers also bought*" section, and your book may be promoted on an "*Amazon recommends*" email. The key to making sales on Amazon is to increase all downloads whether paid for or free. There are many websites that will promote your book as a free download, some require a few days notice and others will only accept books that already have good reviews.

Many self-publishing companies that offer retail and distribution as part of their service provide additional promotional tools for the writer because the more sales you make the more money they make. One of these tools is the author page, make best use of this to publicize yourself as well as your books. These are used by readers and therefore offer you a valuable marketing tool.

Create a website - you can do this for free and websites can be really easy to set up and maintain. Update regularly to ensure your potential readers come back time and time again. Offer incentives such as a free download related to your subject area. Many writers capture email addresses; if you do this ensure you send emails regularly and only send emails/newsletters that contain relevant and useful information.

Promote yourself on other websites – if you have written a book about steam engines then maybe there are website owners that would welcome an article or blog from you.

Write a blog - this can be on anything that is of interest to you and your readers. It could be about your writing day including any frustrations and successes. It could be on anything that is going on in the world. It could include reviews of books you have read. The main point is blog regularly, once a fortnight at a minimum.

Use social media - Facebook, Twitter and Pinterest all provide platforms that enable you to engage with your readers. Sometimes it is suggested that you should not openly promote your wares on social media; you can however say "*really excited about publishing my new book title on Amazon today.*" or "*received an excellent review.*" Manage your time carefully when you engage with any internet activity as you can soon find that five minutes has become an hour.

Consider setting up a social media or website page in the name of your book character; ensure you make it clear this is a fictional character; this can be particularly useful if you are writing a series. Again update regularly.

Create opportunities to promote your book to groups of people – give a talk to an interest group, arrange book signings, do a reading, volunteer, or offer your book as a prize in a raffle. Make use of any opportunity to raise the profile of yourself and your book.

Local radio stations and newspapers are only too happy to interview local people with something interesting to say. Think about what you want to say; will it be about the characters in your book, your previous life, why you write or what are you working on now.

Advertise - this can be expensive with limited payback so look for reasonably priced or free advertising opportunities in locations that are frequented by your potential readers. This might include buying cheap online space or using a small local newsletter.

Contact your local shop – if your book has local interest, don't forget you are a local writer, ask your local shop to stock your book on a sale or return basis; create a poster or leaflet to promote both the book and the shop.

Contact historical sites and tourist attractions – if your book includes a location of historical interest, e.g. a manor house, perhaps they will stock it on a sale or return basis.

At this stage you need to allocate a proportion of your time to actively promoting your book. Immediately after publication this may be as high as 80% of your time. Plan your strategy and undertake the high return activities first. Monitor the results of each activity to ensure you make best use of your time. Incidentally just because it appears that an activity did not make you sales you will have raised the profile of your book – the sales may come later. Note these activities in terms of exposure to possible/probable readers.

At some stage in the near future you will need to reduce the amount of time spent on promotion and allocate this time to writing your next book because the more books you have published the greater your earning potential.

7 - What next?

You've published your book, undertaken some promotional activities and are watching sales grow; what should you do next?

1) Write your next book.
 - Get this done as quickly as possible to stay in the flow and maximise sales and income from your growing reputation. If readers like your book they will want more.

2) Continue to promote your book at every opportunity.
 - Use your free days on KDP Select.
 - Blog.
 - Do book signings.
 - Give talks to local, and national, groups.

The keys to continued success are never stop and never give up. If your promotional activity is not working then try something else. If your next book is not progressing then start a new project and come back to it later. Take a holiday however, if the holiday is a total break from writing, take no longer than a week else you will find it harder to get back to the job of writing and the writing business.

And finally!

Start now. Follow the steps in Publish it! and make your book available to readers. Very soon you will start experiencing the excitement, joy and financial benefits as your book is purchased and enjoyed.

If you would like further hints and tips on developing your career as a writer then follow my blog at:

http://www.writepublishsell.blogspot.co.uk/

Here you will find up to date information on latest trends, advice on writing, ideas for your books, and how technology can help you write, publish and sell your work.

Also by Adam Jackson
Kindle and printed editions available on
Amazon

Write it!
How to write your book in 30 hours or less
Adam Jackson

Whether you are a published writer or just starting out on your writing journey Write it! will provide you with an approach that supports you getting your writing done.

The digital revolution has changed the publishing scene for writers and readers alike. No longer is the reader restricted to those books a publisher deems fit for the market. Writers can now reach markets that were previously closed to them opening up a whole host of opportunities to become a part-time or full-time writer earning an income that reflects their efforts.

If you are ready to start working towards becoming a published writer then Write It! is the perfect guide to writing your book fast. In just 30 hours you could have your work ready for publication. Depending on how much time you commit to writing you could become a published writer in just one week from now.

You will be able to:
 - Identify your time thieves and create the time to write.
 - Set up an effective office with the minimum of equipment.
 - Generate an endless list of ideas; in fact you will never be without an idea again.
 - Plan your book using a method that best suits your way of working.
 - Write fast. Never again be sat at a computer wondering what to write next.
 - Edit your work to ensure readers not only want to read your book but will come back time and time again for more.

This method can be used each and every time you write a book, or any other piece of written work, enabling you to start working from home and building up your writing business.